Angels are Forever

Compiled by Esther L. Beilenson

Illustrated by Jenny Faw

PETER PAUPER PRESS, INC.
WHITE PLAINS, NEW YORK

Copyright © 1994
Peter Pauper Press, Inc.
202 Mamaroneck Avenue
White Plains, NY 10601
ISBN 0-88088-787-7
Printed in Hong Kong
7   6   5   4   3   2

INTRODUCTION

Angels, whether inhabitants of heaven or earth, are a guiding presence in our lives. They give us confidence, comfort us and help keep us safe.

These heartfelt quotes from literature, religious

scriptures, and current-
day angelologists help
us celebrate these celes-
tial beings. Let them
inspire you to reach out
to your guardian angels
and experience the joys
they can bring!

ANGELS
ARE FOREVER

Angel is the only word in
the language which
never can be worn out.

VICTOR HUGO

You don't have to study
to become an angel—
just wing it!

NICOLE BEALE

Our spirits soar on the
wings of angels.

SARAH MICHELLE

Where love abounds,
angels hover overhead.

ANONYMOUS

Where there's peace on
earth, there are angels in
the heavens.

ANONYMOUS

[Communication with angels] starts if you recognize they're there.

MURRAY STEINMAN

It is to those who perceive through symbols, the poets, the artists, and seekers for meaning, that the angel makes himself known.

THEODORA WARD

For he shall give his
angels charge over thee,
to keep thee in all thy
ways.

PSALMS 91:11

It is not because angels
are holier than men or
devils that makes them
angels, but because they
do not expect holiness
from one another, but
from God alone.

WILLIAM BLAKE

Millions of spiritual
  creatures walk the
  earth;
Unseen, both when we
  wake and when
  we sleep.

JOHN MILTON

Angels and ministers of
grace defend us.

WILLIAM SHAKESPEARE

The light that shines on the blessed angels is the supernatural knowledge of God's essence that is a gift of God's grace.

MORTIMER ADLER

[Angels are full of warmth and joy,] and they always say the same thing—*Don't be afraid.*

SOPHY BURNHAM

If you don't marry an
angel, be prepared to
have a devil of a time.

ANONYMOUS

In heaven an angel is
nobody in particular.

GEORGE BERNARD SHAW

Man was created a little
lower than the angels,
and has been getting a
little lower ever since.

JOSH BILLINGS

I will give thanks to you,
O Lord, with all my heart;
in the presence of the
angels I will sing your
praise.

PSALMS 138:1

So in a voice, so in a
shapeless flame
Angels affect us oft, and
worshipped be.

JOHN DONNE

Everyone, no matter
how humble he may be,
has angels to watch over
him. They are heavenly,
pure and splendid, and
yet they have been given
us to keep us company
on our way.

POPE PIUS XII

Since angels are men,
and live together in
society like men on
earth, therefore they
have garments, houses
and other things familiar
to those which exist on
earth, but, of course
infinitely more beautiful
and perfect.

EMANUEL SWEDENBORG

Beware of people who resemble angels, for even the most gentle souls sometimes sprout horns.

SARAH TOWNSEND

If an angel were to tell us anything of his philosophy I believe many propositions would sound like 2 times 2 equals 13.

G. C. LICHTENBERG

When I see angels in
pettycoats I'm always
sorry they hain't got
wings so they kin quietly
fly off whare thay will be
appreshiated.

ARTEMUS WARD

Sing like an angel and the world will sing with you.

ELIZABETH DEANE

See, I am sending an angel ahead of you to guard you along the way ...

EXODUS 23:20

Silently one by one, in
the infinite meadows
of heaven
Blossomed the lovely
stars, the forget-me-
nots of angels.

HENRY WADSWORTH
LONGFELLOW

I think it's one of the scars in our cultures that we have too high an opinion of ourselves. We align ourselves with the angels instead of the higher primates.

ANGELA CARTER

Man is neither angel nor Brute, and the unfortunate thing is that he who would act the angel acts the Brute.

PASCAL

Reputation is what men
and women think of us;
character is what God
and the angels know of
us.

THOMAS PAINE

We are like children, who stand in need of masters to enlighten us and direct us; and God has provided for this, by appointing his angels to be our teachers and guides.

SAINT THOMAS AQUINAS

To angels, home is not
only where the heart
is—but all hearts.

KAREN GOLDMAN

While shepherds
  watch'd their flocks
  by night,
All seated on the ground,
The Angel of the Lord
  came down,
And glory shone around.

NAHUMTATE

If men were angels, no government would be necessary. If angels were to govern men, neither external nor internal controls on government would be necessary.

JAMES MADISON

The soul should always
stand ajar, ready to
welcome the ecstatic
experience.

EMILY DICKINSON

We cannot part with our friends; we cannot let our angels go.

RALPH WALDO EMERSON

Always be an angel-on-call for a friend.

ANONYMOUS

Do not forget to entertain strangers, for by so doing some people have entertained angels without knowing it.

HEBREWS 13:2

The garments of the angels correspond to their intelligence. The garments of some glitter as with flame, and those of others are resplendent as with light: others are of various colors, and some white and opaque.

EMANUEL SWEDENBORG

Angels are wonderful
and exciting, and they
have the appeal of
beings who will take
care of us and manifest
God's personal concern.

ANDREW M. GREELEY

[Angels] are not merely forms of extraterrestrial intelligence. They are forms of extra-cosmic intelligence.

MORTIMER ADLER

Angels exist through the eyes of faith, and faith is perception. Only if you can perceive it can you experience it.

JOHN WESTERHOFF

Angels are reassurance
that the supernatural
and the realm of God
are real.

RICHARD WOODS

If people want to get in touch with their angels, they should help the poor.

LAWRENCE CUNNINGHAM

When angels guide my brush, something heavenly oft appears.

ANGELA HOUSE

An angel can illumine
the thought and mind of
man by strengthening
the power of vision, and
by bringing within his
reach some truth which
the angel himself con-
templates.

SAINT THOMAS AQUINAS

Giving the devil his due
will always jostle the
angels.

ISABELLE LOMOLIN

What! Giving again?
   I ask in dismay,
And must I keep giving
   and giving away?
Oh, no, said the angel
   looking me through,
Just keep giving till the
   Master stops giving
   to you.

*From an English
blacksmith's diary*

Every man contemplates
an angel in his future
self.

RALPH WALDO EMERSON

What might appear as
an angel may be your
love in disguise.

ANONYMOUS

An angel stood and
met my gaze,
   Through the low door-
   way of my tent;
The tent is struck, the
vision says;—
   I only know she came
   and went.

JAMES RUSSELL LOWELL

It felt as if angels were pushing.

ADOLF GALLAND,
*on his first flight in
a jet aircraft*

The angels . . . regard
our safety, undertake
our defense, direct our
ways and exercise a
constant solicitude that
no evil befalls us.

JOHN CALVIN

Time is man's angel.

JOHANN CHRISTOPH
VON SCHILLER

The angels may have wider spheres of action and nobler forms of duty than ourselves, but truth and right to them and to us are one and the same thing.

EDWIN HUBBELL CHAPIN

The very same thing
happened to me in the
first few weeks of my
pontificate, but then one
day my guardian angel
appeared to me in a
daydream and whisper-
ed, *Giovanni, don't take*

yourself so seriously.
And ever since then I've
been able to sleep.

POPE JOHN XXIII,
to a new bishop
suffering from insomnia

Hold the fleet angel fast
until he bless thee.

NATHANIEL COTTON

Marry an angel and
you'll be on Cloud 9.

PHYLLIS D'APRILE ALSTON

There are four corners
    of my bed,
There are four angels
    at my head,
Matthew, Mark, Luke,
    and John,
Bless the bed I sleep
    upon.

A CHILD'S PRAYER

There was a pause—
just long enough for an
angel to pass, flying
slowly.

RONALD FIRBANK

What is man, that thou art mindful of him? and the son of man, that thou visitest him? For thou hast made him a little lower than the angels, and hast crowned him with glory and honor.

PSALMS 8:4-5

God made the angels to
show him splendour.

ROBERT BOLT

The angels are so enamored of the language that is spoken in heaven, that they will not distort their lips with the hissing and unmusical dialects of men, but speak their own, whether there be any who understand it or not.

RALPH WALDO EMERSON